Junior Drug Awareness

Junior Drug Awareness

Valium
& Other Downers

Introduction by BARRY R. McCAFFREY
Director, Office of National Drug Control Policy

Foreword by STEVEN L. JAFFE, M.D.
Senior Consulting Editor,
Professor of Child and Adolescent Psychiatry, Emory University

Cindy Dyson

Chelsea House Publishers
Philadelphia

CHELSEA HOUSE PUBLISHERS
Editor in Chief Stephen Reginald
Production Manager Pamela Loos
Director of Photography Judy L. Hasday
Art Director Sara Davis
Managing Editor James D. Gallagher
Senior Production Editor LeeAnne Gelletly

Staff for VALIUM AND OTHER DOWNERS
Project Editor Therese De Angelis
Contributing Editor James D. Gallagher
Associate Art Director Takeshi Takahashi
Picture Researcher Patricia Burns
Designer 21st Century Publishing and Communications, Inc.
Cover Illustrator/Designer Keith Trego

Cover Photo © Gabe Palmer/The Stock Market

The Chelsea House World Wide Website address is
http://www.chelseahouse.com

3 5 7 9 8 6 4 2

Library of Congress Cataloging-in-Publication Data
Dyson, Cindy.
Valium and other downers/Cindy Dyson.
    pp.   cm. — (Junior drug awareness)
Includes bibliographical references.
Summary: Discusses the use and abuse of various
"downer" drugs, examining why people take them, their
effects on the body, and how to get help.
ISBN 0-7910-5206-0 (hc)
1. Sedatives—Juvenile literature. 2. Tranquilizing drugs—
Juvenile literature. 3. Diazepam—Juvenile literature.
4. Drug abuse—Juvenile literature. [1. Sedatives. 2. Tran-
quilizing drugs. 3. Drug abuse.] I. Title. II. Series.
HV5822.B3D97   1999
362.29'9—dc21   99-25825
                                                              CIP

CONTENTS

by Barry R. McCaffrey
Director, Office of National
Drug Control Policy

Staying Away from Illegal Drugs, Tobacco Products, and Alcohol

Good health allows you to be as strong, happy, smart, and skillful as you can possibly be. The worst thing about illegal drugs is that they damage people from the inside. Our bodies and minds are wonderful, complicated systems that run like finely tuned machines when we take care of ourselves.

Doctors prescribe legal drugs, called medicines, to heal us when we become sick, but dangerous chemicals that are not recommended by doctors, nurses, or pharmacists are called illegal drugs. These drugs cannot be bought in stores because they harm different organs of the body, causing illness or even death. Illegal drugs, such as marijuana, cocaine or "crack," heroin, methamphetamine ("meth"), and other dangerous substances are against the law because they affect our ability to think, work, play, sleep, or eat.

If anyone ever offers you illegal drugs or any kind of pills, liquids, substances to smoke, or shots to inject into your body, tell them you're not interested. You should report drug pushers—people who distribute these poisons—to parents, teachers, police, coaches, clergy, or other adults whom you trust.

Cigarettes and alcohol are also illegal for youngsters. Tobacco products and drinks like wine, beer, and liquor are particularly harmful for children and teenagers because their bodies, especially their nervous systems, are still developing. For this reason, young people are more likely to be hurt by illicit drugs—including cigarettes and alcohol. These two products kill more people—from cancer, and automobile accidents caused by intoxicated drivers—than all other drugs combined. We say about drug use: "Users are losers." Be a winner and stay away from illegal drugs, tobacco products, and alcoholic beverages.

Here are four reasons why you shouldn't use illegal drugs:

- Illegal drugs can cause brain damage.
- Illegal drugs are "psychoactive." This means that they change your personality or the way you feel. They also impair your judgment. While under the influence of drugs, you are more likely to endanger your life or someone else's. You will also be less able to protect yourself from danger.
- Many illegal drugs are addictive, which means that once a person starts taking them, stopping is extremely difficult. An addict's body craves the drug and becomes dependent upon it. The illegal drug–user may become sick if the drug is discontinued and so may become a slave to drugs.

- Some drugs, called "gateway" substances, can lead a person to take more-dangerous drugs. For example, a 12-year-old who smokes marijuana is 79 times more likely to have an addiction problem later in life than a child who never tries marijuana.

Here are some reasons why you shouldn't drink alcoholic beverages, including beer and wine coolers:

- Alcohol is the second leading cause of death in our country. More than 100,000 people die every year because of drinking.
- Adolescents are twice as likely as adults to be involved in fatal alcohol-related car crashes.
- Half of all assaults against girls or women involve alcohol.
- Drinking is illegal if you are under the age of 21. You could be arrested for this crime.

Here are three reasons why you shouldn't smoke cigarettes:

- Nicotine is highly addictive. Once you start smoking, it is very hard to stop, and smoking cigarettes causes lung cancer and other diseases. Tobacco- and nicotine-related diseases kill more than 400,000 people every year.
- Each day, 3,000 kids begin smoking. One-third of these youngsters will probably have their lives shortened because of tobacco use.
- Children who smoke cigarettes are almost six times more likely to use other illegal drugs than kids who don't smoke.

If your parents haven't told you how they feel about the dangers of illegal drugs, ask them. One of every 10 kids aged 12 to 17 is using illegal drugs. They do not understand the risks they are taking with their health and their lives. However, the vast majority of young people in America are smart enough to figure out that drugs, cigarettes, and alcohol could rob them of their future. Be your body's best friend: guard your mental and physical health by staying away from drugs.

WHY SHOULD I LEARN ABOUT DRUGS?

Steven L. Jaffe, M.D., Senior Consulting Editor,
Professor of Child and Adolescent Psychiatry,
Emory University

Your grandparents and great-grandparents did not think much about "drug awareness." That's because drugs, to most of them, simply meant "medicine."

Of the three types of drugs, medicine is the good type. Medicines such as penicillin and aspirin promote healing and help sick people get better.

Another type of drug is obviously bad for you because it is poison. Then there are the kinds of drugs that fool you, such as marijuana and LSD. They make you feel good, but they harm your body and brain.

Our great crisis today is that this third category of drugs has become widely abused. Drugs of abuse are everywhere, not just in rough neighborhoods. Many teens are introduced to drugs by older brothers, sisters, friends, or even friends' parents. Some people may use only a little bit of a drug, but others who inherited a tendency to become addicted may move on to using drugs all the time. If a family member is or was an alcoholic or an addict, a young person is at greater risk of becoming one.

Drug abuse can weaken us physically. Worse, it can cause

permanent mental damage. Our brain is the most important part of our body. Our thoughts, hopes, wishes, feelings, and memories are located there, within 100 billion nerve cells. Alcohol and drugs that are abused will harm—and even destroy—these cells. During the teen years, your brain continues to develop and grow, but drugs and alcohol can impair this growth.

I treat all types of teenagers at my hospital programs and in my office. Many suffer from depression or anxiety. A lot of them abuse drugs and alcohol, and this makes their depression or fears worse. I have celebrated birthdays and high school graduations with many of my patients. But I have also been to sad funerals for others who have died from problems with drug abuse.

Doctors understand more about drugs today than ever before. We've learned that some substances (even some foods) that we once thought were harmless can actually cause health problems. And for some people, medicines that help relieve one symptom might cause problems in other ways. This is because each person's body chemistry and immune system are different.

For all of these reasons, drug awareness is important for everyone. We need to learn which drugs to avoid or question—not only the destructive, illegal drugs we hear so much about in the news, but also ordinary medicines we buy at the supermarket or pharmacy. We need to understand that even "good" drugs can hurt us if they are not used correctly. We also need accurate scientific knowledge, not just rumors we hear from other teens.

Drug awareness enables you to make good decisions. It allows you to become powerful and strong and have a meaningful life!

The drugs known as downers, which are usually taken in pill form, can help relieve a number of medical problems. However, sedatives and tranquilizers can also be dangerous or even fatal when they are not taken according to direction.

1

DOWNERS AND THEIR DISCOVERY

Cassey Fleming sat on a plane flying from Florida to San Diego. Once she arrived, Cassey would undergo a surgery that could change her life. Cassey has epilepsy, a disease that sometimes causes her to lose consciousness and her muscles to spasm.

Suddenly, turbulence made the plane lurch under Cassey. Her body jerked. She blacked out and collapsed against the plane's seat as a seizure took control of her body.

Cassey was only seven years old, but she'd been dealing with epilepsy for five years. So had her mom, Evie Windham. As soon as she saw Cassey begin to convulse, Evie dug into her purse for the syringe filled with **Valium,** a drug used to control **epileptic seizures**. Evie knew that if Cassey didn't get the drug immediately, the seizure could go on for hours, leaving Cassey with brain damage or even killing her.

Struggling to hold her daughter still, Evie sunk the needle into Cassey's arm and pushed. The Valium-filled syringe emptied and within seconds, Cassey's body stopped jerking. Half an hour after receiving the shot of Valium, Cassey felt almost like herself again.

Cassey is 12 years old now, and the surgery has helped her condition. She doesn't have as many seizures, and the ones she does have aren't as bad. In fact, her mother doesn't even have to keep a syringe of Valium in her purse anymore. But Evie is grateful that the drug was there when Cassey needed it. "I think it's a miracle drug," Evie said. "It saved my little girl's life."

Valium is in a group of **sedative** medicines commonly referred to as **downers**. All types of people use downers for all sorts of reasons; controlling epileptic seizures is just one of them. Most times downers are prescribed to help people overcome stress- or anxiety-related disorders such as **insomnia, phobias,** and **panic attacks**. They are also used to treat simple conditions like severe muscle spasms from injuries. These drugs can seem to work miracles, but their misuse can also cause suffering and even death.

What Are Downers?

"Downers" is a slang term for sedative or tranquilizing drugs. Think of downers as "slow-motion" drugs, because they are designed to slow down the functions of the mind and body. In scientific terms, downers are **psychotherapeutic drugs**. That is, they are designed to help people deal with neurological, psychological, and emotional problems. These problems can cause physical disabilities such as sleeplessness, seizures, **hyperactivity**, or severe anxiety.

In this book we will discuss two general types of psychotherapeutic drugs: sedatives and **minor tranquilizers**. Sedatives, such as **barbiturates**, help people sleep. They are often called sleeping pills, but their medical name is **sedative-hypnotics**. Common sedatives include Seconal (nicknamed "reds"), **Quaalude** ("ludes"), and Veronal.

Minor tranquilizers relax or calm people. They are often called **anti-anxiety drugs** because they help people who are extremely anxious or fearful cope with everyday life. A group of drugs called benzodiazepines are the primary type of minor tranquilizer used today. Benzodiazepines include Valium, **Librium, Rohypnol,** and Xanax; minor tranquilizers are sometimes nick-named "tranks" or "happy pills."

A third type, called major tranquilizers, are a group of drugs known as antipsychotics. These drugs are not considered downers; they are prescribed to treat people with **psychotic disorders** or severe depression. Common major tranquilizers are Thorazine and Resperidol.

All downers are synthetic, which means they are created in a laboratory by combining chemicals rather than taken from or made from parts of plants or animals. Downers are also mainly prescription drugs. This means that a doctor must prescribe the drug before a person can buy the drug legally. Downers come in many forms: powders, syrups, drops, capsules,

People who are having trouble sleeping may use sedatives. The most common sleeping pills are a type of drug called barbiturates. These drugs are also known as sedative-hypnotics.

tablets, suppositories, and injectable liquids. Most, however, are pills.

Every drug usually has a chemical name, a generic name, and a brand name. The chemical name of a drug is used by scientists to describe its molecular structure. Its generic name is established by the United States Adopted Names Council. The drug's brand name is determined by the company that makes it; this name is capitalized and usually short and catchy so people will remember it.

Earliest Drugs

Scientists have discovered evidence that people living thousands of years ago took drugs to help them with a variety of problems. Back then, drugs came from natural sources such as plants and animal parts. One of the earliest known books describing natural substances used to treat sicknesses is more than 4,000 years old. It was compiled by a Chinese emperor. The Egyptians, and later the Greeks, also kept detailed writings about how to prepare drugs from plants and animals.

The most powerful drug the ancient Egyptians and Greeks used was probably **opium**, which is derived from the opium poppy. Opium relaxes muscles and eases pain; it can also create a euphoric feeling sometimes known as a "high." Heroin and morphine are both made from opium. A statue thought to be 3,500 years old shows three poppy seed pods nestled in the headdress of a smiling woman whose eyes are closed. This statue and later texts about how to prepare opium from opium poppies are the earliest known signs that people from ancient times made and used drugs to relax. In medieval times, alcohol became another popular relaxation and sleeping drug.

In other parts of the world, people used drugs created from a variety of plants to help them relax. The kind of plants they used depended on what was native to their region; the most common included chamomile, lavender, passionflower, valerian, and rosemary. Take a walk through the tea aisle in your grocery store and you'll see that we still use many of these same plants to help us relax.

Miracle Elixirs

In the 1700s, "miracle cures" known as elixirs were developed and peddled by traveling salesmen, many of whom had little or no medical training. If you were suffering from, say, sleeplessness, these itinerant sales- men would recommend a concoction such as Ma Munn's Elixir of Opium, Dr. Ryan's Worm Destroying Sugar Plums, or Lydia Pinkham's Vegetable Tonic For Female Problems. These so-called medicines promised to cure nervous disorders, sleep problems, digestive disorders, rashes, and all sorts of other ailments.

Most cure-alls of the 1700s, 1800s, and early 1900s contained alcohol, opium, or **cocaine**, a dangerous drug that increases the heart rate. Laudanum, one of the most popular elixirs of the 19th century, was made from opium and wine mixed with spices. The two drugs not only made people feel sluggish and dull, but they also caused **addiction** in users.

Overdoses of such drugs were sometimes lethal. Lucy Henderson was a child in 1846, traveling by wagon train along the Oregon Trail with her family. She learned firsthand how deadly these medicines could be:

Mother had brought some medicine along. . . . My little sister, Salita Jane . . . got the bottle and drank it all. Presently she came to the campfire where Mother was cooking supper and said she felt awful- ly sleepy. . . . When Mother tried to awake her later she couldn't arouse her. Lettie had drunk the whole bottle of laudanum. It was too late to save her life.

The scientific name of this plant is *Papaver somniferum,* but most people know it as the opium poppy. The juice of this poppy has painkilling and sleep-inducing properties. Opium can be processed into other drugs, such as morphine, which has medical uses, and heroin, which is an illegal and dangerous substance.

A Scientific Breakthrough

An important improvement in sedative drugs came in 1863, when a 29-year-old Belgian researcher named Adolph von Baeyer formulated the first of a group of drugs called barbiturates. Barbiturates slow the activity of the **central nervous system**,

How Did Barbiturates Get Their Name?

Adolph von Baeyer created a new substance when he combined two acids, malonic acid and urea (a white acid excreted by mammals after they digest proteins). The new substance looked interesting, and von Baeyer rushed to a local tavern to celebrate his discovery. When he arrived, he found a group of army officers celebrating the feast day of St. Barbara, the patron saint of artillerymen and people who work with explosives. Von Baeyer named his discovery "barbiturates," combining the name "St. Barbara" with the chemical name "urea."

thereby decreasing anxiety and producing a feeling of well-being. But von Baeyer's discovery was not recognized until 42 years later, when two German scientists, Emil Hermann Fischer and Joseph von Mering, were looking for a drug to treat people suffering from anxiety and insomnia. They discovered that barbiturates could help, and by changing the chemical combination of von Baeyer's substance just slightly, they synthesized a new drug, which was named barbital. The drug was sold under the name Veronal.

Veronal quickly became popular. In 1912, seven years after Veronal was invented, researchers synthesized another barbiturate called phenobarbital (whose brand name is Solfoton). This drug is still on the market.

Early Uses of Barbiturates

In the early days of barbiturate use, the drugs were often called "truth serums" because medical doctors thought that they decreased a person's inclination to lie. Barbiturates did seem to make some users more truthful, but most people who used them were just as likely to chat about fantasies and dreams as they were about facts. As scientists learned more about what barbiturates could and could not do, using them as truth-inducing substances fell out of practice.

By the 1930s, psychiatrists prescribed barbiturates for patients undergoing psychotherapy. They believed that patients who felt sleepy during therapy were more willing to be treated. Patients undergoing "sleep therapy" were drugged with barbiturates for an average of 11 days at a time. But as psychatrists increased their use of barbiturates, they discovered that patients coming out of therapy had often become **physically dependent** on the drugs and suffered from **withdrawal** when their prescription was discontinued. As a result, the practice of using barbiturates during psychotherapy was eventually abandoned.

Since the first barbiturates were introduced in the early 1900s, researchers have synthesized hundreds of similar substances. Only a few of the original ones made it to the market, but these proved effective in treating a variety of disorders. Barbiturates soon became the most popular prescription drugs in history. However, as their popularity grew, the dangers of overusing this class of drugs became more apparent.

Discovering the Dangers

From the beginning, there were signs that barbiturates had harmful side effects. The first clues came from Germany after the drugs were introduced in the early 1900s. Several people died when they deliberately took

One of the common uses of downers such as Librium is to relieve feelings of depression. Only medical doctors can advise you about whether you should take prescription medications. Never take any kind prescription drug without a doctor's approval.

overdoses. Others took so much of the drug over a long period of time that they became severely disoriented for days or weeks on end.

By the 1940s in the United States, the dangers of barbiturates were well known—but abuse of these drugs had already become widespread. Using barbiturates for recreational purposes (to get high or relax) had become so popular that they were often called "thrill pills." By the 1950s, this kind of use had become an acceptable practice for adults. The practice spread to college students and teens in the 1960s; young people could often get supplies of the drugs very easily by taking them from their parents' medicine cabinets. It became common to combine barbiturates with other drugs to heighten or enhance the effects of the other drugs.

Barbiturate abuse became so common during these decades that in some countries it was the number-one cause of drug deaths. In the mid-1950s, for example, 70 percent of the people taken to poison treatment centers in Copenhagen, Denmark, had overdosed on barbiturates.

Losing Popularity

In the 1970s, as newer drugs were developed to treat anxiety and insomnia, barbiturate use slowed. By 1984, barbiturates were called "has-been" drugs in a report on adolescent drug use in the *American Journal of Public Health*. Still, this category of drugs was linked to nearly one-third of all drug-induced deaths at that time.

Why did barbiturates lose popularity in the United States? The discovery of better and more effective downers played a part, but at the same time, the U.S. government also began to tighten control of the drugs. In 1973, the Drug Enforcement Agency changed the regulations that governed how barbiturates could be prescribed. Drugs in the United States are classified into five "schedules," depending on their potential for abuse and the dangers of their effects. Schedule I drugs are described as having a high potential for abuse, having no currently accepted medical use in the United States and being unproved for use in medical situations. These drugs can be legally used only under strictly controlled research conditions. (Schedule I drugs include heroin, LSD, and marijuana.) Schedule V drugs are the least harmful and can be purchased at drug and grocery stores without a prescription.

When laws regulating barbiturates were tightened, most of them were moved from Schedule III to Schedule II, placing them in the same category as addictive drugs like morphine and cocaine. Although a drug listed as Schedule II can be prescribed by physicians, the prescription can be filled only if the patient presents the written prescription in person to the pharmacist who is filling the order. No prescription refills are allowed with Schedule II drugs. A few other barbiturates are classified as Schedule III or IV, meaning that they require a doctor's prescription but are subject to fewer restrictions.

Discovering Tranquilizers

What were these new drugs that helped reduce barbiturate use? They were the family of drugs classified as minor tranquilizers. The most common drug in this family is called Valium.

Minor tranquilizers were discovered in a roundabout way. In 1955, Dr. Leo Sternbach, a chemist employed by a large drug company called Hoffman-LaRoche, synthesized a compound that he ultimately believed would be unsuccessful in treating anxiety. He stored the substance in his lab and forgot about it. That's where it stayed until two years later, when the drug was

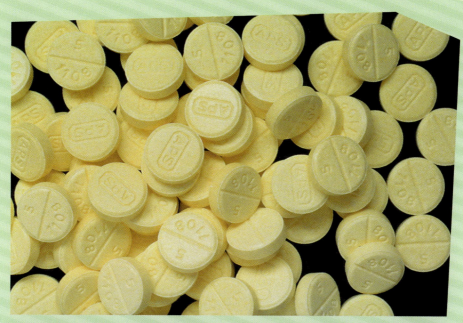

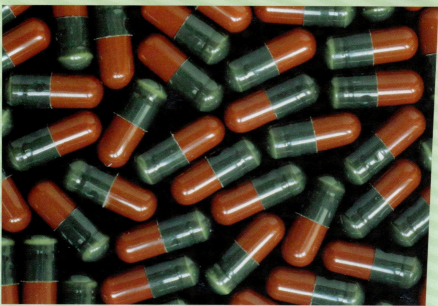

These photos show the minor tranquilizers Valium (top) and Librium (bottom). Both belong to the drug class known as benzodiazepines, and are useful in relieving anxiety, relaxing muscles, and treating convulsions.

rediscovered while technicians were cleaning the lab. Researchers didn't think the new drug would amount to much, but they decided to run a few tests on it anyway.

To their surprise, the drug seemed to calm the lab animals they tested it on. Wild monkeys became so tame that they could be handled by researchers. The scientists also discovered that the new drug helped to relax the animals' muscles and prevented convulsions.

As researchers studied the drug more closely, they found that Sternbach had been wrong about the kind of drug he thought he had developed. This new drug was in the **benzodiazepine** family. It was named chlordiazepoxide and marketed under the name Librium. Before long, doctors were prescribing it widely to treat anxiety.

Several other drugs in the benzodiazepine family were synthesized soon after. Although they vary in some ways—the size of the dose, how quickly they act, how long they remain in the body—they are very similar to one another. The most well-known of these drugs is **diazepam,** sold under the brand name Valium. Hundreds of benzodiazepines have been synthesized since the 1950s, and a few are still on the market.

Tranquilizer Explosion

During the 1960s and 1970s, Valium and Librium were extremely popular. In fact, benzodiazepines were the most-prescribed drugs in the United States during much of the 1960s. The drugs did not cause the grogginess that barbiturates had. Moreover, the risk of overdose was low, and dependency and addiction were virtually unheard of with these new drugs.

As a result, people began taking them for all sorts of minor problems that can often be treated without drugs. For example, a homemaker might complain to her doctor that she felt bored and fidgety. Chances were she'd be prescribed a drug like Valium. A college student who worried about his grades might be advised to take tranquilizers.

Not until the late 1970s did the first hints appear that these drugs also had side effects and risks. A number of television reports focused on people who had trouble trying to stop taking the drugs; the reports also displayed how easy it was for people to get prescriptions to these pills in the first place. In 1979, a woman named Barbara Gordon published a book called *I'm Dancing as Fast as I Can* about the physical, mental, and emotional trauma she experienced when she abruptly stopped taking Valium after having abused it for years.

Just as with barbiturates years earlier, reports of tranquilizer addiction and withdrawal multiplied and its use decreased. Many physicians who had originally prescribed tranquilizers for a wide variety of complaints began reserving their use for patients with severe anxiety or insomnia.

How do drugs like barbiturates and tranquilizers cause addiction? What makes them dangerous when those who take them are not carefully monitored? In the next chapter, we'll examine what these drugs do to the body and brain.

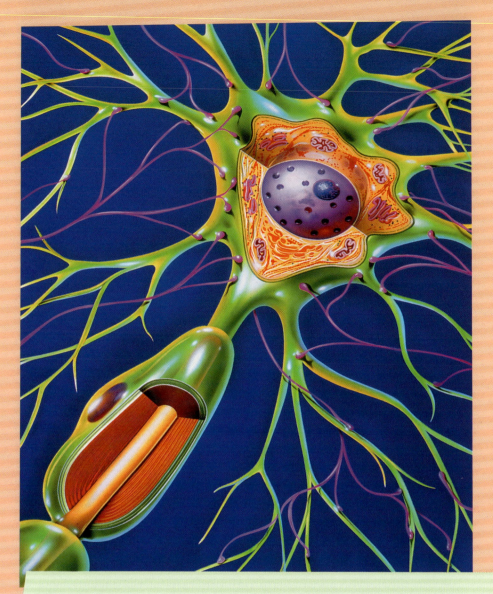

This illustration shows a nerve cell, or neuron. The cell body is the purple mass at the top right. The neuron receives messages from other neurons through dendrites (the green tentacles). Messages go out from the nerve cell via a single axon, which is on the lower left. Other neurons communicate with this one through the pink branches leading to dendrites. (The tiny spaces between the tips of the pink branches and the dendrites can be seen in the next illustration.)

INSIDE BODY AND MIND

Most psychotherapeutic drugs either slow down or speed up a bodily function such as breathing or muscle contractions. But while these drugs are very powerful, there are many things they cannot do. For one thing, drugs can't make the body do things that it couldn't do before. For example, they can't make a body fly or breathe water.

Downers (minor tranquilizers and sedatives) work by slowing down the rate at which a person's nerve cells communicate with each other. When nerve cells are working in slow motion, a person reacts more slowly to outside stimuli.

The Central Nervous System

Underneath your skin is a network so complex that no one knows exactly how it works. It's called your

nervous system, and without it you wouldn't survive.

Your nervous system is divided into three parts: central, peripheral, and autonomic. The **peripheral nervous system** is the entire nervous system outside the brain and spinal cord. It is made of nerve cells bundled into cables that run from each part of your body—your eyeball, pinkie, toe, or elbow—to your spinal column and brain. The autonomic nervous system is part of the peripheral system, and it regulates the involuntary functions of internal muscles and glands. Controlling all of these is the central nervous system, which is made of nerves in your brain and spinal cord. Nerve cells in your peripheral system report to nerve cells in your central system about what is going on around you and inside you.

Billions of nerve cells live within your central nervous system. Millions of messages about what's happening inside and outside your body travel through your central nervous system every minute.

The nerves cells are strung together like beads of a necklace. Each cell has to pass messages to the next nerve cell in line. This process has to continue with each cell before the brain can find out what's going on.

To play this game of pass-it-on, nerve cells rely on branch-like structures called **axons**. These axons reach out toward neighboring cells that are ready to receive and transmit messages. Axons carry messages away from the cell. Another kind of branch, called a **dendrite**, carries messages toward the cell. Cells are lined up so the axon of one cell almost touches the dendrite of the next. The cells don't quite touch; the

A close-up of a synapse, a tiny gap between neurons by which special chemicals called neurotransmitters carry messages. The area of the receiving neuron that takes up the chemical substance is called a receptor site (shown in orange).

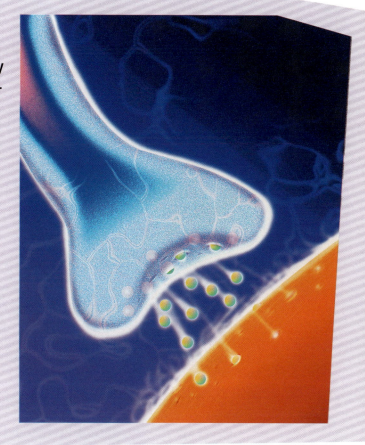

tiny gaps in between are called **synapses**.

So how does a message make it to your spinal column and then your brain when it has to get across all those synapses? It does so through chemicals called **neurotransmitters**. Neurotransmitters act like bridges between nerve cells.

Here's how it works. You stub your toe on a door jamb. Before you even feel any pain, a nerve cell in your toe has to "tell" the nearest nerve cell what has happened. That first nerve cell sends a neurotransmitter from its axon into the synapse between it and the next cell in the chain.

To get the message across, the neurotransmitter has to "plug itself in" to the dendrite of the second nerve cell. Fortunately, the dendrite comes with many, many different sized plug-ins called **receptors**. The neurotransmitter simply finds the receptor that corresponds to the pain you're feeling and links up with it. The same thing happens over and over until the message reaches your brain. You yell, "Oooowwww!" and hop around on one foot while holding the throbbing toe.

All this happens very, very fast. Think about how fast it takes between the time you stub your toe and the time you feel the pain. During that time, a million neurotransmitters have passed on a million messages through the nerve cells between your injured toe and your brain.

Benzodiazepines in Action

How do downers like benzodiazepines work within the nervous system? Simply put, these drugs help natural neurotransmitters work better.

Scientists believe a neurotransmitter called **gamma-aminobutyric acid** (**GABA** for short) is nature's way of calming overactive nerves. GABAs are found in the brain and spinal cord. These neurotransmitters tell the nerves to quiet down. GABAs are always ready for action in the body, but sometimes they are not enough to calm the nerves completely.

That's what sedatives and tranquilizers do. They help GABAs do their job. How? By making it easier for GABAs to fit into receptors on nerve dendrites.

When downers reach the central nervous system, they immediately rush into nerve synapses. When they're plugged in, a strange thing happens: the receptors next to them change. Think of these receptors reshaping themselves, making the GABAs fit more easily into the plug-ins. Presto! More GABAs are plugged into more nerve cell receptors. Pretty soon, nerves quiet down and the body relaxes.

Scientists think the body must supply its own kind of anti-anxiety drug, another neurotransmitter that helps GABA slip into plug-ins. But so far, this natural downer has yet to be found.

Where the Work Is Done

Most of this neurotransmitter activity goes on in the **limbic system**. The limbic system consists of several structures that lie deep within the brain at the top of the brain stem, which enters the skull from the top of the spine. It's a very primitive area of the brain; even simple animals like frogs have limbic systems. That leads scientists to think that this part of the brain evolved early in the history of life.

The limbic system is responsible for emotions, such as fear and anxiety. When researchers destroyed parts of the limbic systems of fearful, aggressive monkeys, they became tame. On the other hand, when researchers stimulated the limbic systems in normal rats, the rats acted fearful and defensive.

All this leads scientists to think that benzodiazepines make it easier for GABAs to work in the limbic system. With more GABAs working, it seems, a person quickly becomes less fearful and anxious.

The Trips Downers Take

After a downer is swallowed, the pill enters the stomach, where it is broken down and its parts are released into the small intestine. Once there, the drug is absorbed into the bloodstream. From the bloodstream, most of the drug migrates to the limbic system.

The drug stays in the limbic system for as few as 15 minutes to as long as several days, working in the nerve synapses. The drug is then **metabolized**, or removed from the bloodstream, by the liver. Then, it is either passed out of the body in the urine or stored in the body's fat cells.

Some sedatives and tranquilizers stay in the body much longer than others. If a person takes another dose of such drugs during this time, the amount that was already in the body combines with the new dose. Such double dosing can result in an **overdose**.

Dependence and Withdrawal

Both sedatives and minor tranquilizers can cause physical dependence, a condition that can occur when a person has been taking an addictive drug for a long time. After a while, the body adapts to require regular doses of the drug and has trouble functioning without it. Sedatives, especially barbiturates, can quickly lead to dependence, but even mild tranquilizers may produce dependence. Like the body, the brain also becomes dependent on the drug to function properly. Obtaining it becomes very important to the user—sometimes it even takes over that person's life. This is called addiction.

As the body becomes dependent on a drug, it also develops a **tolerance** to the substance's effects. This means that the user must take greater and greater

Drug addiction is a brain disease. Using addictive drugs causes physical changes in the brain that require the person to continue taking the drug in order to function normally. In experiments with laboratory rats that are given regular doses of addictive drugs like heroin or cocaine, scientists find that the rats will change their behavior to keep receiving the drugs. The rats will no longer seek food or the company of other rats. Instead, they will continuously press a bar that injects cocaine or heroin into their brains and bodies. Sedatives and tranquilizers are also addictive, and they can affect the brain in the same way as cocaine or heroin.

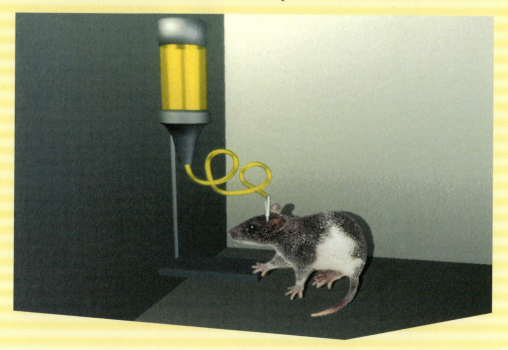

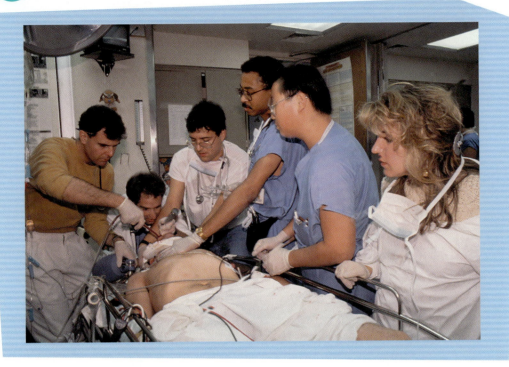

Many people who misuse sedatives and tranquilizers wind up in the hospital suffering from an overdose. It is especially easy to overdose on barbiturates. Unfortunately, some people who do so do not survive.

amounts of the drug in order to achieve the same effect once provided by a smaller dose. A person who has abused a drug for years may develop a tolerance so high that he or she can take amounts that would kill someone who has never used the drug before.

Let's say, for example, that Mr. A has been taking a barbiturate for several months. As his body develops a tolerance to the drug, the mellow feeling Mr. A gets from the drug doesn't last as long as it did when he first started taking the pills. He used to be able to take a pill before going to bed and get eight hours of sleep before the drug's effects wore off. But after several months of taking the drug, the pill keeps him asleep for only six hours.

Mr. A may start taking two pills rather than one so he can sleep longer. For a while that works, but his body's tolerance level adjusts again, and soon he needs three pills to sleep soundly for eight hours.

Let's say Mr. A realizes that he has become physically dependent on his sleeping pills, and he knows he is taking doses that are too high. He decides to quit **cold turkey**—to stop taking the pills completely rather than taper off. Because his body now requires regular high doses of the drug, he will go through a state known as withdrawal and will suffer from a variety of unpleasant symptoms.

How severe a person's withdrawal symptoms are depends on how long the person has been taking a drug, how large the doses are, and how long the drug stays in the person's body. For someone who has been using sedatives or minor tranquilizers heavily for a long period of time, withdrawal can be fatal.

People who are dependent on sedatives or minor tranquilizers usually feel excitable and fearful when they quit. They may shake, lose their appetites, and feel that their hair is standing on end. More severe reactions include shakiness, rigid muscles, weight loss, convulsions, delirium, hallucinations, and very high fevers. If the person's system for regulating blood pressure breaks down, he or she can die. In these cases a benzodiazepine, such as Valium, is administered to the person to try to prevent death.

Overdosing

What if Mr. A just keeps taking more and more pills to keep sleeping eight hours a night? Eventually, he'll overdose.

A drug overdose occurs when a person either deliberately or accidentally takes a greater amount of some

Downers can be especially dangerous if the user drinks alcohol while taking them. Both tranquilizers and alcohol depress, or slow down, a person's bodily functions. When these two kinds of drugs are used together, they may slow down breathing and heart rate enough to kill the person.

substance than the body can handle. This second way of overdosing often occurs with people who use illegally manufactured drugs. Because illegal substances are not carefully regulated, their strength and purity vary widely and the user may not realize how great an amount he or she has taken until it is too late.

Deadly Combinations

Because tranquilizers and alcohol work in similar ways, their combined effects can be dangerous. The combination of even one Valium pill and a couple of alcoholic drinks can cause a person to overdose. In fact, the combined effects of these two drugs are so powerful that taking them together can cause death.

An extreme overdose of any drug depresses the central nervous system. Breathing slows and reduces the amount of oxygen in the blood. The body becomes colder or warmer, heartbeat slows, and blood pressure falls. Shock can set in. If a person doesn't make it to a hospital in time, he or she could die.

Doctors and psychiatrists sometimes prescribe a benzodiazepine such as Xanax for a person suffering from major depression. Sedatives and tranquilizers are also prescribed to treat anxiety and insomnia, as well as to treat epilepsy and the symptoms of alcohol withdrawal.

DOWNERS AT WORK

At one time, sedatives and minor tranquilizers were commonly used to treat depression. However, the development of another type of drug called an **antidepressant** is now more commonly prescribed than sedatives and minor tranquilizers to treat depression.

Anxiety

The most common use for downers is treating people who suffer from excessive anxiety. A certain amount of anxiety is normal and very common; all of us experience it at one time or another. In fact, feeling some level of anxiety is physically helpful. Let's say you feel nervous about performing in an upcoming soccer game. As you think about the game, your body produces extra **hormones** called **epinephrine** and

norepinephrine. These are sent into your bloodstream to make you more alert, more ready to move. That extra alertness may not feel good. It may make your stomach fluttery and your hands sweat. But once you get on the playing field, it may help you play better.

But when anxiety interferes with a person's ability to work, study, or complete simple tasks, that person may have a condition called **anxiety disorder**. Psychiatrists divide anxiety disorders into two main types: phobic disorders and **generalized anxiety disorders**.

Phobic disorders can be either a **simple phobia** or **agoraphobia**. Simple phobias are the most common. They affect about 7 percent of women and 4.3 percent of men during any six-month period. Simple phobias are fears of specific things. These phobias include claustrophobia (the fear of closed in spaces) or mysophobia (the fear of dirt or germs).

The second kind of phobic disorder, agoraphobia, is a fear of being helpless or embarrassed without having a way to escape the situation that is causing these feelings. People with agoraphobia may feel vulnerable and helpless in public places and open spaces, and so they avoid these areas. Many agoraphobics suffer from panic attacks.

A panic attack usually comes on suddenly. A person suffering from such an attack will have trouble breathing. Her heart rate increases, and she begins to sweat heavily. She may even feel like she's about to die. A person who has a panic attack may later feel afraid of

The most common use for downers is treating people who suffer from severe anxiety. There are two types of anxiety disorders: phobic and generalized anxiety. A minor tranquilizer can help people with severe anxiety disorders overcome their physical symptoms.

the kind of place where the attack occurred. Some people who have had these attacks become so afraid of having another one that they won't leave their homes.

The second broad category of anxiety disorder is called generalized anxiety. Let's say a man feels jittery, tired, and nervous most of the day. From time to time, his heart pounds; he sweats and his hands get clammy. His stomach churns, and he has to urinate often. The man can't concentrate or sleep well. He has a constant feeling that something terrible is about to happen. He is suffering from generalized anxiety.

About 3 to 5 percent of adults have this disorder at some time in a given year. It often begins in adolescence and flares up in times of severe stress. But it nearly disappears at other times.

Minor tranquilizers can help people with severe anxiety disorders overcome these physical symptoms. However, minor tranquilizers are no longer the primary drug used to treat anxiety. Doctors prefer a type of drug called **selective serotonin-reuptake inhibitors** (SSRIs) to treat the problem. This group includes Prozac, Zoloft, Paxil, and Luvox. But drugs are usually only part of the cure; the other part is counseling and psychotherapy.

Insomnia

Sleeping disorders are the second most common problem for which people take downers. The drugs most often prescribed for sleep disorders are benzodiazepines like Valium and Librium and barbiturates like Solfoton. Doctors usually prescribe barbiturates for sleep problems that have occurred over a period of less than two weeks. For more severe problems, doctors usually prescribe a benzodiazepine.

Alcohol Withdrawal

Just as with any other drug, when people whose bodies have become dependent on alcohol stop taking it, they experience withdrawal symptoms. The effects of alcohol withdrawal usually include shaky muscles, heavy sweating, hallucinations, and convulsions about 12 to 48 hours after a person quits drinking alcohol. Several days after the convulsions have stopped, an even worst withdrawal symptom—**delirium tremens**—develops. During the "DTs," as they're called, temperature and blood pressure can rise so greatly that the alcoholic can die.

If the person gets to a treatment center or hospital before the DTs set in, an injection of a tranquilizer like Valium, Librium, or Ativan can prevent the DTs from starting.

Muscle Relaxation

Downers, particularly the minor tranquilizers, are also used to ease neuromuscular disorders, such as tight muscles. This condition can arise from a number of different physical problems, including strychnine poisoning, **tetanus** infection, **multiple sclerosis**, and simple muscle strain.

Poisoning by strychnine (the active ingredient in substances like rat poisons) and infection with the tetanus bacteria (which can occur with puncture wounds) can make muscles so tense that the person is unable to breathe. A tranquilizer, if given quickly and continuously through the illness, can keep a person breathing and alive.

People who suffer from multiple sclerosis, a disease that affects nerves and muscles, are sometimes prescribed downers to ease stiffness. One of the side effects, however, is grogginess from the high dose required.

Sedatives and tranquilizers can help treat people with psychological disorders. However, these drugs work best when combined with psychotherapy or counseling.

Epilepsy

Tranquilizers can help keep alive people who have certain kinds of epileptic seizures. Epilepsy is a genetic disorder marked by episodes of uncontrolled, chaotic electrical activity in the brain. This kind of activity alters consciousness and causes involuntary movements. An estimated 50 million people worldwide have epilepsy. The disorder usually strikes from the ages of 2 to 14. In the worst cases, a person can die or be left with brain damage.

The drugs most commonly prescribed for epilepsy are anti-convulsant drugs. However, as the story of Cassey in chapter 1 showed, Valium can also be helpful in treating seizures.

Surgery

Before some patients are wheeled into surgery, they get so nervous that it can be hard to administer the anesthesia that will put them to sleep during the procedure. Benzodiazepines can help with this problem. These downers are called **anesthetic** sedatives. Although barbiturates were once used to put people to sleep before they underwent surgery, today only a few barbiturates are used, and only for very short surgeries, like pulling teeth.

Sedatives and minor tranquilizers have many medical uses. However, many new drugs, such as anti-convulsants and SSRIs, are less likely to be misused or abused and are more effective in treating specific conditions. As a result, in recent years physicians have prescribed fewer sedatives and minor tranquilizers than in previous decades.

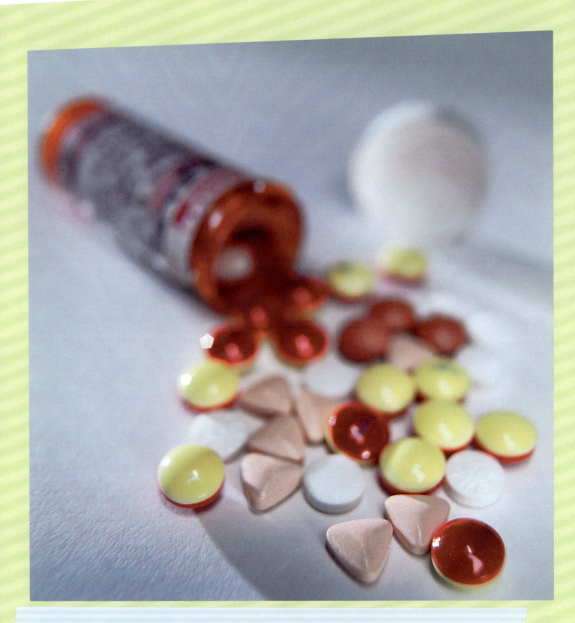

Most people don't think of downers as being dangerous like heroin or cocaine are. However, any drug, even if it is prescribed by a doctor, has the potential to cause serious health problems—even death—if it is misused.

MISUSES
AND ABUSES

People don't abuse downers to the extent that they abuse other drugs, such as cocaine or alcohol. But that doesn't mean that these drugs are never abused at all.

The most common abuse pattern goes something like this. Let's say a woman has a Valium prescription to treat her anxiety disorder. After she takes the pills for a few months, she finds that she needs to take more to get the same relaxed feeling she once had with the proper dose. So she takes one extra pill each day. A few months later, she starts to take a second extra pill every day. Soon she's taking much more than her doctor ordered. She has formed a dependence on that drug.

The woman is physically dependent on Valium, but she is not an addict. She doesn't feel good if she misses a dose, but she doesn't spend a lot of time trying to find more Valium or rearranging her life so that she can spend more time taking the drug.

Of course, some people become seriously dependent on downers, especially on barbiturates. These people may resort to breaking the law to get more drugs and spend a good part of their day feeling groggy or sleeping. To get enough of the drug, they may visit several doctors, getting a prescription from each one. Or they may forge prescriptions or steal from hospitals and pharmacies to get enough downers to satisfy their dependence.

Some people who abuse downers take them with illegal drugs like cocaine, opium, or amphetamines. Downers either intensify the effects of these drugs or they decrease the jittery feeling that results from cocaine or amphetamine use. Such drug combinations were most popular in the 1960s and 1970s, and they led to a dramatic increase in the number of deaths from drug overdoses.

Twenty years ago, about 1 in 10 teenagers had tried each of the three most common kinds of downers by the time he or she graduated from high school. In the 1950s and 1960s, downers were so popular with adults that one in seven used them. It would take the over-dose deaths of several famous people before Americans began to realize how deadly these drugs could be. One such celebrity was Marilyn Monroe, a famous movie star of the 1950s, who died in 1962 by taking all the prescribed barbiturates in her medicine cabinet. Another star, Jimi Hendrix, a popular rock guitarist in

Barbiturates and benzodiazepines are legally available only by prescription from a physician. However, some people who become dependent on these drugs try to cheat the system. They may forge prescriptions or go to several doctors to get many prescriptions for the same drug.

the 1960s, died in 1970 after combining barbiturates and alcohol.

These high-profile deaths, along with new medical studies showing the dangerous of downers, taught doctors that these drugs should be more carefully prescribed. By the 1980s, sedative and tranquilizer use had fallen dramatically.

Jimi Hendrix (center) is considered by some to be the greatest rock guitarist of all time. Although he was a brilliant musician, he was not so intelligent when it came to drugs. A heavy drug user, Hendrix died in 1970 at age 27 after taking an overdose of barbiturates.

Illegal Downers

Only two common benzodiazepines (minor tranquilizers) are illegal in the United States: **methaqualone** (Quaaludes) and Rohypnol.

Methaqualone hit the U.S. drug market in the mid-1960s and quickly became popular with people looking for a "safe" high. However, the drug was far from safe. Many people overdosed and died on the drug. It was particularly dangerous when mixed with alcohol. In 1982, methaqualone was categorized as a Schedule I drug, making it illegal to use except in controlled scientific research. Unfortunately, large amounts of the drug are still being smuggled into the United States, primarily from Columbia.

Rohypnol has been used in Europe since the 1970s and is also available by prescription throughout most of South America. Until 1996, small quantities could be brought into the United States to treat patients with anxiety.

"Roofies," as the drug is often called, act much like Valium but pack 10 times the power. During the first half of the 1990s, it gained popularity with teens in Florida and Texas. The drug, especially when mixed with alcohol, can make a person feel drunk very quickly; it also makes people forgetful and compliant. Rohypnol has been named in several cases of rape, in which it was allegedly slipped into victims' drinks before the rapes to make them give in and then make them forget what had happened.

While on tour in Rome, former Nirvana leader

Do Kids Use Downers?

Abuse of sedatives and tranquilizers is not as common among young adults as abuse of other drugs like alcohol, tobacco, and marijuana. About 3 percent of all youths ages 12 to 17 have used downers illegally, compared to 40 percent who have tried alcohol or tobacco and 20 percent who have tried marijuana.

Kurt Cobain overdosed after taking a mix of heroin, Rohypnol, and champagne. Doctors pumped his stomach and saved his life, but one month later, he committed suicide by overdosing on other drugs. Cobain's use of sedatives and his decision to kill himself may not be related, but using anti-anxiety drugs sometimes depresses people so greatly that it can lead to suicidal feelings and thoughts.

Portrait of a Drug Abuser

Chances are you will never have a friend who takes sedatives or tranquilizers. Studies show that teens don't use or abuse these drugs very often. Only about 2.9 percent, or about 3 out of 100 kids ages 12 to 17 have ever taken downers without a doctor's prescription. Meanwhile, 40 percent of teens have tried cigarettes and 40 percent have tried alcohol. Almost 20 percent, or one in five, have tried marijuana.

Teenagers don't seem to enjoy the sleepy, mellow feelings downers cause as much as adults do. Some experts say that the feeling may seem boring to youngsters. Even among teens who used downers, the drugs' effects seem less important to them than the reason they are taking the drugs. In a study of teens who regularly used sedatives, the teens said they used them to escape reality or to shock their parents, for example. Most said that they took so much that they didn't remember the experience the drug produced anyway.

The people who seem to have the most difficulty with abuse of anti-anxiety drugs are the elderly. Studies show that such drugs last longer in the bodies of elderly people and that they tend to use the drugs for longer periods of time. Both of these factors make senior citizens more likely to abuse the drug unintentionally.

Although drug dependence can be treated, the best way to stay drug-free is never to start using these substances in the first place.

ENDING DRUG ABUSE

I f someone is using an illegal drug like heroin, he or she is abusing the drug. There is no medical reason for a person to use a drug like this. However, defining abuse of legal drugs such as sedatives and tranquilizers is not so easy. Distinguishing between legitimate use and abuse can be difficult, not only for the person taking the drug but also for the person's friends and family. After all, the drug user is usually taking the drug to relieve a medical or psychological problem and not to get high.

That's why it's best if a doctor or drug abuse expert speaks with and observes a person who is suspected of abusing tranquilizers or sedatives. But how do you know when to call in an expert?

Signs of Downer Abuse

Watch for these signs if you suspect someone is taking too much of a prescribed sedative or tranquilizer.

A person may be groggy or fall asleep at unusual times, like during class or at lunch. He or she may have trouble walking. Some people have sudden personality changes and becoming unusually aggressive, angry, or even violent.

If you know someone taking a sedative or tranquilizer who shows these signs, encourage the person to see his or her doctor. Your friend may simply need to switch to a different kind of prescription drug or a lower dose of the same drug.

You may also notice when a person suddenly stops taking a prescribed anti-anxiety drug. He or she may have trouble sleeping, feel overly anxious, shake, and sweat a great deal. Once again, encourage the person to see a doctor.

Treatment for Drug Abuse

When a person is extremely dependent upon a specific drug, a treatment program can save the user's life. The kind of treatment that works best depends on the type of drug being abused, the length of abuse, and the abuser.

Treatment falls into two general categories: behavioral therapy and drug therapy. Behavioral treatments include counseling, psychotherapy, support groups, and family psychotherapy. Drug therapy involves giving abusers decreasing amounts of either the drug being abused or a similar drug. The process of gradually removing drugs from a person's system is called **detoxification**.

Older people are more likely to abuse sedatives and tranquilizers than young adults. However, their abuse is usually unintentional. If you think someone you know is taking too much of a prescription drug, urge your friend or loved one to see a doctor.

Treatment can be conducted on an outpatient basis or as part of a residential program. Outpatient programs, in which the patient lives at home but attends regular treatment sessions, usually stress counseling. They work best for people who have stable lives with

How Can I Tell If Someone I Know Has a Drug Problem?

Most people who are having difficulties with drugs will not ask for help. In fact, a drug abuser is more likely to deny the problem and try to hide the symptoms. The person may be embarrassed or afraid to confide in someone else. Still, there are some warning signs that you can look for if you suspect that a friend or loved one is abusing alcohol or other drugs. If someone you know displays one or more of the following traits, he or she may have a drug problem:

- Getting high or getting drunk on a regular basis
- Lying about the amount of alcohol or other drugs he or she uses
- Avoiding you or other friends to get high or drunk
- Giving up activities such as sports, homework, or hanging out with friends who don't drink alcohol or use other drugs
- Having to drink more alcohol or use increasing amounts of another drug to get the same effect previously achieved with a smaller amount

jobs and family, and have only a short history of drug abuse.

Residential treatment is a highly structured program in which patients live in a special treatment center for several months. These programs usually work best for people with long histories of abuse, people who have become involved in crimes because of drug use, and people who have family problems or who lack close social ties. They focus on helping a person develop and maintain a more healthy lifestyle.

- Constantly talking about drinking alcohol or using other drugs
- Pressuring other people to drink alcohol or use other drugs
- Believing that one cannot have fun without alcohol or other drugs
- Getting into trouble with the law or getting suspended from school for an alcohol- or other drug-related incident
- Taking risks, including sexual risks or driving under the influence of alcohol or other drugs
- Feeling tired, run-down, hopeless, depressed, or even suicidal
- Missing work or school or performing tasks poorly because of alcohol or other drug use

Keep in mind that some of these signs, such as poor job or school performance and depression might be signs of other problems. They could also be symptoms of an illness that you may not know about. Be sure to talk to an adult you trust or who is trained to recognize alcohol and other drug abuse. A parent or other adult family member, or a doctor, nurse, religious leader, school counselor, or coach can give you advice about what to do next.

Another kind of residential treatment is a **chemical dependency unit**. This type of program usually lasts three to six weeks and focuses on getting the patient through withdrawal and breaking psychological addiction. It is usually followed by outpatient treatments, such as therapy or a Twelve Steps program like the one used by Alcoholics Anonymous or Narcotics Anonymous.

Most treatment programs include three phases. In the first, the patient must break dependence and manage his or her withdrawal from drugs. The second phase

The best way to overcome drug dependence is to seek treatment.
These teens are participating in a group counseling session to
help them learn how to stay drug-free.

requires breaking psychological habits while finding
ways to avoid one's desire to use drugs. The third phase
involves creating a newly focused life with rewarding
work, relationships, and educational opportunities that
decrease the chance that the person will return to an
addict's way of life.

Treatment for Overdose

Treatment for drug overdose has a different goal than treatment for overcoming addiction. The goal of overdose treatment is more immediate: to save a person's life.

The most important part of keeping an overdose patient alive is to keep the person breathing. In hospitals and clinics, most overdose patients have their stomachs pumped to remove as much of the drug as possible from the body and to decrease the amount of the drug the person can absorb. If breathing becomes difficult, patients are given oxygen.

With today's treatment methods, only about 1 out of 100 people who overdose on sedatives die after reaching a hospital or clinic in time.

Prevention

Experts estimate that drug abuse costs the United States $67 billion a year—the total cost incurred by drug-related crimes, medical care, drug treatment, welfare programs, and time lost from work.

The best solution to this problem, of course, is to stop people from abusing drugs in the first place. That's why local schools and communities and the federal government put such great effort into drug education and prevention programs. Studies show that for every $1 spent on drug prevention, communities can save $4 to $7 in drug abuse and treatment costs.

Prevention programs teach children and adults how to prevent drug abuse. They show how certain risk

Close family relation-
ships can help young
adults resist the lure of
drugs. Many prevention
programs focus on
teaching parents how to
talk with their children
about the dangers of
drug and alcohol abuse.

factors can make people more likely to try drugs or
alcohol. These factors include a chaotic home life,
parents who abuse drugs, a tendency to get into trouble
with authorities, a lack of strong positive friendships,
poor performance in school, and association with people
who use drugs or with places where drug use is accepted.

Factors that help children avoid using drugs include
doing well in school, having positive, drug-free friends,
being involved in school and religious activities, and
understanding how drugs are harmful. Parents who

know what their children are doing at all times, enforce clear rules about drug use and other behaviors, and stay involved with their childrens' lives help to prevent drug abuse.

The best prevention programs also give children the tools they need to resist the lure of drugs. Programs work best when they're repeated several times. That's why many schools employ drug prevention programs from primary school through high school.

Treatment for Anxiety

Many people with free-floating anxiety (anxiety not related to a specific event or cause) rely on behavioral therapy. There are three basic types of behavioral therapy: biofeedback, desensitization, and anxiety management training.

People who use **biofeedback therapy** learn how to monitor their feelings of anxiety using skin temperature as a guide. In this way, they learn to gain some control over their autonomous nervous system, which automatically regulates bodily functions such as breathing and heart rate.

Desensitization therapy helps people deal with a specific anxiety—a fear of elevators, for example. People learn techniques to make themselves relax and lower their heart rates. Next, they confront their fears in small steps. For example, a person who is afraid of elevators may first try looking at a picture of an elevator, then walk by one, and eventually ride a real elevator without feeling fear.

One of the best ways to stay healthy and drug-free is to get plenty of exercise. When you feel fit and full of energy, you're less likely to put harmful substances into your body.

Anxiety management training works like desensitization therapy, except that patients are taught to deal with general anxiety symptoms by using techniques to relax.

Protect Yourself

Do you feel pressured to try downers or other kinds of drugs? If so, you're not alone. About one in six teens report being asked to take a drug during any given month.

The best way to deal with such pressure is to avoid it. If people you know are using drugs, try not to associate with them. If you know drugs will be available at a friend's house or at a party, stay away by finding other activities to keep you busy. And if you do go, be sure that you can say no when offered alcohol or other drugs. Find friends who share your views about drugs and who also want to avoid using them.

If you go to a party and then discover that people are using drugs, it might be a good idea to leave. If you do decide to stay, be aware of what is going on around you, and never leave your drink unattended or try a substance that you're unfamiliar with or that is offered by someone you don't know or trust.

If you do know someone who is abusing or selling drugs, tell your parents, school officials, or a counselor. You will not only be helping yourself; you'll also be helping your friends and classmates.

Drugs are powerful substances that can save lives—but they can also kill when abused or used improperly. Using certain drugs the right way and for the right reasons can make the difference between being drug-dependent and staying healthy and happy.

GLOSSARY

addiction—a condition of some drug users that is caused by repeated drug use. A drug user's body develops a tolerance to the drug and needs increasingly large amounts of the drug to achieve the same level of "high." An addict continues to take the drug despite severe negative consequences. Obtaining and using the drug take over the person's life. When a person who is addicted to a drug stops taking the drug, withdrawal occurs.

agoraphobia—an abnormal fear of being helpless in an embarrassing or inescapable situation. Agoraphobia is characterized by the avoidance of open or public places.

anesthetic—a drug that causes a loss of feeling or consciousness.

anti-anxiety drug—a drug that helps to prevent or relieve anxiety by decreasing activity in the central nervous system.

antidepressant—any of a number of drugs used to relieve symptoms of depression.

anxiety disorder—a psychological or physical illness that causes a person to experience abnormal levels of uncertainty, fear, and tension.

anxiety management training—a non-drug treatment for anxiety that teaches patients how to relax when dealing with general anxiety symptoms.

axon—an extension of a nerve cell that conducts impulses away from the cell body.

barbiturate—any one of a category of sedative drugs that decrease activity in the central nervous system. Barbiturates are generally used to treat insomnia, anxiety, and neuro-muscular disease.

benzodiazepine—any of a group of drugs, called minor tranquilizers, that are used to treat insomnia, anxiety, and neuromuscular disease.

biofeedback therapy—a treatment program that uses special machines to make a person aware of unconscious or involuntary bodily processes, such as heartbeats or brain waves. The therapy allows the patient to gain some control over the body's responses to anxiety or stress.

central nervous system—the core of the human nerve system, made up of the brain and spinal cord.

chemical dependency unit—a center for short-term drug treatment that helps people deal with recovery from drug abuse and the withdrawal symptoms that accompany it.

cocaine—a powerful and illegal stimulant made from the leaves of the coca plant and usually sold as a white powder. Cocaine is highly addictive.

cold turkey—a slang term used to describe the act of abruptly and completely quitting an addictive drug.

delirium tremens (DTs)—violent hallucinations, with convulsions or tremors, that are induced by abusing alcohol over an extended period.

dendrite—a branch-like structure on a neuron that receives messages from other parts of the body.

desensitization therapy—a method used to treat anxiety in which a person gradually faces his or her fears by confronting situations that induce the emotion.

detoxification—the process of removing drugs or other chemicals from the body. Also, any treatment program designed to help a person complete that process.

diazepam—a drug in the benzodiazepine family, considered a minor tranquilizer and marketed under the brand name Valium.

downers—a slang term for drugs that have a calming effect, help reduce anxiety, and can induce sleepiness. Barbiturates, sedatives, and tranquilizers are considered downers.

epileptic seizures—convulsions triggered by disturbances of the electrical signals in the central nervous system.

epinephrine—also called adrenaline, a chemical released by the body during stressful situations that causes the heart to beat more rapidly.

gammaaminobutyric acid (GABA)—a neurotransmitter that decreases neuron activity.

generalized anxiety disorder—a condition in which a person experiences extreme anxiety that is not linked to a specific event or situation.

hormone—a substance produced by a gland in the endocrine system and carried by the blood to body organs and tissues. Hormones regulate some body functions and control growth. Synthetic hormones that mimic the effects of natural substances are made in laboratories.

hyperactivity—the state or condition of being excessively or abnormally active.

insomnia—a chronic inability to sleep.

Librium—a trade name for chlordiazepoxide, a minor tranquilizer.

limbic system—the region of the brain that controls emotions and feelings of pleasure. The limbic system is one of the most primitive of brain structures.

metabolize—in a living organism, to change food into energy and living tissue and then dispose of waste material.

methaqualone (Quaalude)—a sedative-hypnotic drug once prescribed for anxiety. Because of its addictive properties, methaqualone is no longer on the market.

minor tranquilizer—any of a group of drugs used to reduce anxiety and tension. Minor tranquilizers are also called anti-anxiety drugs; the most commonly prescribed types are benzodiazepines.

multiple sclerosis—a disabling nervous system disorder that causes partial paralysis.

nervous system—a complex network of cells that receive, transmit, and interpret messages from the body and external sources. The nervous system is controlled by the brain and the spinal cord.

neurotransmitter—a chemical that is released by neurons and carries messages between them.

norepinephrine—a chemical released by the body during stressful situations that causes the heart to beat more rapidly.

opium—one of the drugs derived from the milky juice of the poppy plant. Others include morphine, codeine, and heroin.

overdose—too large a dose, as of a medicine or drug.

panic attack—a sudden onset of symptoms that include difficulty breathing, excessive sweating, elevated blood pressure, and raised heart rate. Panic attacks are caused by psychological, rather than physical, factors.

peripheral nervous system—the part of the nervous system that conducts messages from the body to the central nervous system.

phobia—an abnormal fear or anxiety of a specific situation or thing.

physical dependence—addiction; a state in which a drug user's body chemistry has adapted to require regular doses of the drug to function normally. Stopping the drug causes withdrawal symptoms.

psychotherapeutic drug—a substance used to treat emotional, psychological, and neurotransmitter disorders. Sedatives and tranquilizers are psychotherapeutic drugs.

psychotic disorder—a mental condition in which a person suffers from delusions (such as feelings of paranoia or of persecution) and/or hallucinations (hearing or seeing things that aren't really there).

Quaalude—the brand name for methaqualone, a common sedative and an antianxiety and insomnia drug that was taken off the market because of widespread abuse.

receptor—small areas at the end of each dendrite that are sensitive to specific neurotransmitters. Receptors are essential in passing messages through the nervous system.

residential treatment program—a highly structured drug treatment program in which patients are required to live at the treatment center for extended periods of time.

Rohypnol—a potent minor tranquilizer that is now illegal in the United States; also known as "roofies" or "rope."

sedative—drugs that calm and relax and can induce sleepiness.

sedative-hypnotic—any one of a group of sedatives that will also induce sleep at high doses.

selective serotonin-reuptake inhibitor (SSRI)—any of a group of antidepressant drugs that alter the level of the neurotransmitter serotonin in the brain. SSRIs include Prozac, Paxil, Zoloft, and Luvox.

simple phobia—an abnormal fear or anxiety of a specific thing or situation.

synapse—a gap between neurons by which neurotransmitters carry messages.

tetanus—an infection caused by the toxic excretions of the tetanus bacteria.

tolerance—a condition in which a drug user needs increasing amounts of the drug to achieve the same level of intoxication previously obtained from using smaller amounts.

Valium—the trade name for diazepam, a minor tranquilizer.

withdrawal—a process that occurs when a person who is physically dependent on a drug stops taking the drug.

BIBLIOGRAPHY

Ator, Nancy Almand, and Jack E. Henningfield. *Barbiturates: Sleeping Potions or Intoxicants?* New York: Chelsea House Publishers, 1992.

Bachman, Jerald G., Lloyd D. Johnston, and Patrick M. O'Malley. *National Survey Results on Drug Use from the Monitoring the Future Study 1975–1995.* Washington, DC: U.S. Government Printing Office, 1996.

Balick, Michael J., and Paul Alan Cox. *Plants, People, and Culture: The Science of Ethnobotany.* New York: Scientific American Library, 1996.

Bird, Stephen, and B. Joan McClure. *Prozac and Other Anti-depressants.* Philadelphia: Chelsea House Publishers, 2000.

Brodie, Martin J., and Marc A. Dichte. "Drug Therapy." *New England Journal of Medicine,* 18 January 1996.

Clayman, Charles. *The Human Body: An Illustrated Guide to Its Structure, Function, and Disorders.* New York: Dorling Kindersley, 1995.

Department of Health and Human Services. *National Household Survey on Drug Abuse: Population Estimates 1997.* Washington DC: Department of Health and Human Services, 1998.

——. *Preliminary Results from the 1997 National Household Survey on Drug Abuse.* Washington DC: Department of Health and Human Services, 1998.

Family Medical & Prescription Drug Guide. Chicago, IL: Consumer Guide Publications International, 1993.

Long, James W., and James J. Rybacki. *The Essential Guide to Prescription Drugs.* New York: HarperPerennial, 1995.

Miller, Brandon Marie. *Just What the Doctor Ordered: The History of American Medicine*. Minneapolis, MN: Lerner Publications, 1997.

Substance Abuse and Mental Health Services Administration. *Death Count, All Ages, All Races, Both Genders 1995*. Washington, D.C.: Office of Applied Studies, 1996.

Windham, Evie, and Cassey Fleming. Interview by author. Ocoee, FL, 3 November 1998.

Winger, Gail. *Valium and Other Tranquilizers*. New York: Chelsea House Publishers, 1992.

FIND OUT MORE ABOUT VALIUM AND OTHER DOWNERS

The following list includes agencies, organizations, hotlines, and websites that provide information about tranquilizers, sedatives, and drugs of abuse. You can also find out where to go for help with a drug problem.

Many national organizations have local chapters listed in your phone directory. Look under "Drug Abuse and Addiction" to find resources in your area.

Agencies and Organizations in the United States

**American Council
    for Drug Education**
164 West 74th Street
New York, NY 10023
212-758-8060
800-488-DRUG (3784)
http://www.acde.org/wlittlefield

**Center for Substance Abuse
    Treatment**
Information and Treatment
    Referral Hotline
11426-28 Rockville Pike, Suite 410
Rockville, MD 20852
800-622-HELP (4357)

Families Anonymous
P.O. Box 3475
Culver City, CA 90231-3475
310-313-5800
800-736-9805

Girl Power!
U.S. Department of Health and Human Services
Office on Women's Health
11426 Rockville Pike, Suite 100
Rockville, MD 20852
800-729-6686
http://www.health.org/gpower

Just Say No International
2000 Franklin Street, Suite 400
Oakland, CA 94612
800-258-2766

Narconon International
800-468-6933
rehab@narconon.org

Narcotics Anonymous
P.O. Box 9999
Van Nuys, CA 91409
818-780-3951

**National Adolescent Suicide
Hotline**
800-621-4000

**National Center on Addiction
and Substance Abuse
at Columbia University**
152 West 57th Street, 12th Floor
New York, NY 10019-3310
212-841-5200 or 212-956-8020
http://www.casacolumbia.org/home.htm

**National Clearinghouse
for Alcohol and Drug
Information (NCADI)**
P.O. Box 2345
Rockville, MD 20847-2345
800-729-6686
800-487-4889 TDD
800-HI-WALLY (449-2559, Children's Line)
http://www.health.org/

**National Council on
Alcoholism and Drug
Dependence, Inc. (NCADD)**
12 West 21st St., 7th Floor
New York, NY 10017

212-206-6770
800-NCA-CALL (622-2255)
http://www.ncadd.org/

**Office of National Drug
Control Policy**
750 17th Street, N.W., 8th Floor
Washington, DC 20503
http://www.whitehousedrugpolicy.gov/ondcp
888-395-NDCP (6327)

**Parents Resource Institute for
Drug Education (PRIDE)**
3610 Dekalb Technology Parkway, Ste 105
Atlanta, GA 30340
770-458-9900
http://www.prideusa.org/

Shalom, Inc.
311 South Juniper Street, Room 900
Philadelphia, PA 19107
215-546-3470

Agencies and Organizations in Canada

Addictions Foundation of Manitoba
1031 Portage Avenue
Winnipeg, Manitoba R3G 0R8
204-944-6277
http://www.mbnet.mb.ca/crm/health/afm.html

Addiction Research Foundation (ARF)
33 Russell Street
Toronto, Ontario M5S 2S1
416-595-6100
800-463-6273 in Ontario

**Alberta Alcohol and Drug Abuse
Commission**
10909 Jasper Avenue, 6th Floor
Edmonton, Alberta T5J 3M9
http://www.gov.ab.ca/aadac/

**British Columbia Prevention
Resource Centre**
96 East Broadway, Suite 211
Vancouver, British Columbia V5T 1V6
604-874-8452
800-663-1880 (British Columbia only)

Canadian Centre on Substance Abuse
75 Albert Street, Suite 300
Ottawa, Ontario K1P 5E7
613-235-4048
http://www.ccsa.ca/

Ontario Healthy Communities Central Office
180 Dundas Street West, Suite 1900
Toronto, Ontario M5G 1Z8
416-408-4841
http://www.opc.on.ca/ohcc/

Saskatchewan Health Resource Centre
Saskatchewan Health, T.C. Douglas Building
3475 Albert Street
Regina, Saskatchewan S4S 6X6
306-787-3090

Websites

Avery Smartcat's Facts & Research on Children Facing Drugs
http://www.averysmartcat.com/druginfo.htm

D.A.R.E. (Drug Abuse Resistance Education) for Kids
http://www.dare-america.com/index2.htm

Hazelden Foundation
http://www.hazelden.org/

Join Together Online (Substance Abuse)
http://www.jointogether.org/sa/

National Institute on Drug Abuse (NIDA)
http://www.nida.nih.gov

Partnership for a Drug-Free America
http://www.drugfreeamerica.org/

Reality Check
http://www.health.org/reality/

Safe & Drug-Free Schools Program
http://inet.ed.gov/offices/OESE/SDFS

INDEX

PICTURE CREDITS

CINDY DYSON has enjoyed researching topics that capture her attention since she was a young girl. On topics ranging from horses to paleontology, she devoured library books by the dozen. Dyson has turned her desire for information into a job as a freelance magazine writer and book author. She lives in Montana, where she writes regularly about science and other subjects that spark her imagination.

BARRY R. McCAFFREY is Director of the Office of National Drug Control Policy (ONDCP) at the White House and a member of President Bill Clinton's cabinet. Before taking this job, General McCaffrey was an officer in the U.S. Army. He led the famous "left hook" maneuver of Operation Desert Storm that helped the United States win the Persian Gulf War.

STEVEN L. JAFFE, M.D., received his psychiatry training at Harvard University and the Massachusetts Mental Health Center and his child psychiatry training at Emory University. He has been editor of the *Newsletter of the American Academy of Child and Adolescent Psychiatry* and chairman of the Continuing Education Committee of the Georgia Psychiatric Physicians' Association. Dr. Jaffe is professor of child and adolescent psychiatry at Emory University. He is also clinical professor of psychiatry at Morehouse School of Medicine, and the director of Adolescent Substance Abuse Programs at Charter Peachford Hospital in Atlanta, Georgia.